Rattle   Young   Poets   Anthology

EDITOR-IN-CHIEF
Alan Fox

EDITOR
Timothy Green

ASSISTANT EDITOR
Megan Green

EDITOR EMERITUS
Stellasue Lee

COVER ART & DESIGN
David Navas
coverscovered.com

PROOFREADING
Jeffrey Gerretse

Rattle Young Poets Anthology, 2014

www.Rattle.com

CONTENTS

2014

INTRODUCTION

and down they forgot as up they grew
              —E. E. Cummings

There's not a bad poet in first grade. None of them are anything but fresh and original ... they don't know how to avoid being original.
              —Sharon Olds, Rattle #17

... our minds are search engines constantly producing ideas to make an impact on the world, whether it is big or small.
              —E. Wen Wong, page 87

When most people think of "children's poetry," they think of poems written by adults for kids. They don't think of children themselves as poets, and it's very difficult to find any anthologies of poems written in the other direction— by children *for* adults, as well as those their own age. But the early years of language development are magical. No other time in life is full of such wonder, such imagination, and such playfulness. Young poets don't write out of habit. They haven't yet learned how to be cliché. They write with a natural spontaneity that adults can only hope to achieve.

But it's not only older poets that have much to learn from this anthology—these young people have lessons for us all. One of the many things that poetry does is help us see through the eyes of another; this collection teaches us what it feels like to be young in the 21st century, looking ahead at a future in which the stakes are immeasurably large. How does an eight-year-old respond to climate change? How does an eleven-year-old process the notion of a beheading? How does a four-year-old experience her mother's anxiety? These may be kids, but they write about most of the things that adults do, and with a depth of understanding that deserves more respect than they're often given.

This is not a cute collection hoping to win your adoration. These are real poems, by talented authors, with important stories to share—stories that are at turns haunting and hilarious, heart-warming and heart-breaking. Be delighted and inspired, but don't treat these poets lightly.

Timothy Green
October 22nd, 2013

Gwen Allison

THE SHARK SAID

The shark said to the human,
"I'm sorry but I must do this."

The human said to the shark,
"Spare me please."

The shark said to the
human, "You do not understand,
I must do this.

"I need your opinion on wristwatches."

Savannah Alvarez

RAMBUNCTIOUS

Rambunctious is with me
Like literally inside me
I am going crazy and spinning in a tornado
With happy and fun
I hit my head on a tuba
I fill my bathtub with soda
Me and Rambunctious jump in
I make a clay bunny
Write my name on the wall
I play hopscotch with hula-hoops
My ears shrink and I hear a ringing
I jump into a mirror
And ride my bike into a trash can
All this time I have Rambunctious inside me
I erase the board and write everything again
We climb a tree to the top
Then we jump off with a plop
I hit my head on the tuba again
And put some earmuffs on a bear
Then I walk outside and see a cloud
A cloud that is shaped like a cloud
And I stop

LONDON

Dirty brown water cuts this bloody pizza
Clean through
On one side you'll get your head chopped off
On the other your head wobbled and tilted
Looking at skyscrapers with names like
The Gherkin The Shard of Glass The Cheese
Grater. I'll give you a map:

Beefeaters & Beheadings	River	Cheese Graters & Pickles

Fact: London has very different dietary needs.

Cailena Bickell

DON'T WORRY, MOM, DON'T PANIC

If I made up a poem,
I would call it:
"Don't Worry, Mom, Don't Panic."

And,
If I were you,
I would slide down a rainbow.
If I were you,
Mom,
I'd get a bunk bed,
So I wouldn't have to sleep with Dad.

And,
If I'm me,
I'll marry a girl.
Because boys are always being funny with the jokes,
Jokes, jokes, jokes,
All the time.

Like, I know Dad is tricking me,
When he says Aunty Kim doesn't have a heart.
'Cause Aunty Kim loves me
More than anything
In the whole world
And that takes a big heart.
Only bad guys don't have hearts.

Don't worry, Mom,
Don't worry about bad guys,
'Cause Dad is big, and he helps crying people,
And he shoots coyotes that get over the fence to eat us.
Too bad he's too big for the school bus.

I love Dad 'cause he's my dad,
All mine,
And Chloe's,
But she's a baby,
So it's OK to share with her.

And Mom is always like:
"Here's my card,
I'll do some work for you.
I write stories about horses,
And roosters,
And kids,
And work."
But not Elmo,
Never Elmo.

I'm too little,
But too little is not too bad.

And, Mom?
Be careful.
Don't talk to seagulls.
They eat garbage and their breath is stinky.

You don't have to be brave all the time, Mom.
Here,
Hold my hand.
Do you feel better now?

I love you, Mom.
Don't worry, I watch out for birds.
You are the banana in my eye;
You are my best Momma.
And Dad is a hero,
And everybody shouts,
"Yay, Freddy!"

I don't need to go to school today,
I know everything, now.
Oh, but
Mom, Mom, Mom, Mom, Mom,
I don't know anything yet.

But,
Someday,
I'll be a doctor.
And I'll say,
"Uh oh, Mom.
There's a beetle in your boob.
DON'T PANIC."

THE DONKEY

Did you see it, trudging, all day,
along the asphalt road? And in the evening,
opening up its graceful stride—an armful of rime-gray stone,
a stillness even as it cantered into the sureness of its feet,
a snowdrift, a feather of a scrub jay,
pulling its shrill bray into the crackling winter air? Did you hear it,
braying and mourning? A harmony like the ocean
waves lapping at a lion's husky growl?
And did you see it, finally, just under the winter
sun—a gray shadow disappearing along with the sun,
its hooves like stones dropping,
its fur the glistening of a dove's call?
And did you feel it,
in your heart, how to open your hands to them?
And have you revised your heart?

Oscar Brady

THE MOUNTAIN RAVEN

Snow fell on the Mountain Raven
the river gushed over him
he wanted freedom
instead he met a deep sleep
as he fell,
it took him to where
his dreams began
with snow.

BEARER OF THE LIGHT

Oh, bearer of the light,
Bringer of change.
Illuminate the darkest crevices,
Reveal the deepest depths.
Graceful, serene, deadly.
A gliding contradiction.
Slicing through the blackest waters,
Elegant, beautiful, lethal.
A shimmering murderer.
Oh, bearer of the light, swim on.

WHEN PEOPLE LEAVE THIS EARTH

When people leave this earth
Their buildings will crumble
And the vines will creep in.

Dogs will run and play wherever they like.
Cats will hunt and poo on the carpets.
Eagles will nest on the top floors,
Soaring in the deserted concrete jungles.

Tigers would go and lie
In the meat section of the supermarket.

The Earth is alive.
The Earth is going back to the way it was.

FIREFLY

Dipping,
　　dancing,
　　　flying high,
　　　　　beautiful soaring firefly.
　　　　I watch it flicker
　　　　　　as it passes by.

Lauren E. Carter

A GIRL OF FIVE OR EIGHT'S EXEMPLUM

Around the age of
five or eight
a small child snuck into her mother's closet
and stole her most expensive pair of heels.
She smeared pink lipstick across her face
and smiled.
Although the three-sizes-too-big shoes on her feet
and the huge pink grin she wore made her
resemble a clown
she was beautiful.

Around ten or nine
she did the same
but her mother's shoes began to fit
and the lipstick stayed within the lines.
She walked up and down the carpeted hallways
leaving light shoe prints snug into the deep base
while balancing on the needle that supported her few steps
before she fell face first into the shoeprints she had made.

Through years eleven and twelve
instead of adding, subtracting, and dividing worksheets
she added, subtracted, and divided how many more inches
until she was five-foot-eight
with a calculator, of course.

At year thirteen
her mother's heels were replaced by her own
and the pink had turned to dark shades of red
but the smile had faded.
There were too many inches to grow
and too many to lose.
The mirror went from her best friend
to her worst enemy.

But until year twenty-three
she will never realize
she is not a girl
who is in pictures
on her wall.
She will always be a girl
who wore her mother's high heels
and smeared pink lipstick across her face.

Rubio Jett Castagna-Torres

I DOODILYE YOU COO COO

I DOODILEY DOODILYE

YOU I DO YOU

TO AND YOU DO YOU

DOODILYE ME? YOU

DO, OK I DOODILYE YOU DO

I DO SO DO YOU TO

I DO YOU

THE END

BOB THE BEAR

bob the bear breaks himself
and some balls come out
and that lamp comes out
and a daddy comes out
and a hammer comes out
and a nail
and bob the bear
hammered the nail
and fixed himself

SALMON

It should be easy to write art
But it isn't
It should be easy to love you
But it isn't
When we were south of Wales
You yelled at her but she was dead
And now it should be easy
But it isn't

BIG SIS

My big sister is a little creepy
She leaves the faucet sometimes leaky
I think my big sister is Goth
She smells like honey and peanut butter
But somehow I still love her

Jo'lene Dailey

WHAT I WANT TO DO MOST OF THE TIME

It feels like I need
To go to my dad's house
And when I'm at my dad's house
I want to go to my mom's house
I want to be at both houses

Sophia Dienstag

GRANDPA BOB

When Grandpa Bob came back from his first date with my grandma he said
"I'm going to marry Dale, or a woman just like her."
He impressed her with his SAT scores.
He sold his prized stamp collection
To pay for their phone calls.

My mom knows all too well that when he's in a pleasant mood
He cracks jokes
About golf or traveling or my brother's picky eating.
When he's in a lousy mood
He's irritable and grouchy and acts his old age
Always grumbling under his breath.
And whenever we go out to eat
He practically learns our server's life story
He says
"If I was from the Guide Michelin what should I order?"

He has a black bushy mustache
A nose like Cyrano
And glasses as round as the buttons on a polo shirt.

Once little children in a park thought he was wearing a disguise.
He told them he wasn't.
They didn't believe him
But he wasn't exasperated.
He just told the children to try
And take off his nose.

Gabby Dodd-Terrell

HE LIVES IN AN ARK AND DREAMS

My grandfather's afraid of fortune and sails the world
In his handkerchief
He waves to the bottles in the sea
And reads their messages
The trenches are overflowing
It's hard to stay positive
My grandfather's afraid of the sky
His red kite rests on a cenotaph
My grandfather's afraid of silence
He cradles the sound of crows
My grandfather's afraid
Of saying goodbye

Lessons

i remember
standing on a beach
watching a kite fly away over the ocean
and feeling
a wrenching guilt and shame
i remember
refusing to share a candy
with a friend
and watching her face crumple in tears
i remember
standing and watching
red-gold leaves saunter down
and thinking
how is this dying
so beautiful
i do not remember
when i first realized i would die
or that other people felt like i do
or that even the most precious things
can be lost
but these are probably
pretty good guesses

Kofi Edufo

MAKING NOISE

The dead dog snores,
making noise in the world
full of mounds.
I can name two
mounds
belonging to my late friends,
a cat
and a fowl,
whom I feed the sun on the face
I tell a guest at the party,
where little else is eaten.
A man's world he tells me
with a wink, this entire town
today is the kind of memorial day,
collecting shells, deep
and long from the eyes,
home is closer to sunset,
everybody looks at the foot coming back.

SUDAN

Beggars on the streets,
nothing is what they eat.

Selling glasses and socks,
On a board there are lots.

Roads are filled,
Sudan has much to build,
with a donkey on our side,
there is nothing to hide.

The traffic light counts down,
16, 15 even the lights show brown.

Men in white,
Sudan has so much might.

The most important, the Nile,
It may be dirty but it has style.

Now smell it, sniff it,
no lights but it's always lite.

Khartoum Khartoum,
It's like a colorful amazingly amazing room.

So look out of the window and smile,
You have just experienced the Nile.

Phoebe Fischer

YELLOW

Yellow's a smiley-face and a big banana,
a honey-suckle vine and a crayon diorama.
Yellow's a big ol' pile of hay.
Yellow's a happy, happy day.
Yellow's a smile, a toothy grin.
Yellow's a medal an athlete would win.
Yellow's a crayon box and a brand new pencil,
yellow's a happy-face circle stencil.
Yellow's a bright-colored party balloon,
yellow's a person whistling a tune.

EULOGY FOR A BALLOON

A balloon once lived for a month
and a little bit more
until Daddy accidentally murdered him.

But he is still in our hearts.

He was brave to be pushed in the air.
I remember when he made
a little girl laugh so hard
that she screamed.

And this is true.

He traveled with me upstairs
and downstairs. His final trip was upstairs.
I wish I could tell you all the adventures
but the last adventure
you can see
ends here in this chilly sandbox
with sandwiches.

You may eat them.

Aaron Fox

IT'S RAINING

Today
because someone

turned on
the sprinklers

on
top

of
the moon.

SUMMER PEACHES
for Peaches

I don't remember everything,
but I remember summer peaches.
We used to eat them in the condo at the beach
and for a long time,
those were the best peaches I knew.
We had peaches when she came,
and suddenly those Florida fruits meant nothing.
We called her Peaches,
and she was the best one I'll ever know.
She loved all of us—
Our family was hers.
I don't forget the way her eyes softened,
when she saw my father.
And he would say,
"She's one of a kind."
She's in the backyard and the river now,
and no sun shined when she died.
I don't remember everything,
but I remember the smell of her ashes
and I remember summer peaches.

Piper Ginn

THE CHASE

The phone rings ...
She struggles to listen, amidst the rumble of the bus,
the teenage chatter, and the thunderous laughter.
"Mom" her daughter's voice comes, rushed and shaky.
"How's the baby?" she asks, gripping the handrail.
Within a moment, she's tossed into the world
of Down Syndrome.
Down
        Down
                Down
                        she falls.
Down Syndrome—foreign words, scary words,
life-changing words.
Words that someone else should own.
The bus stops, the kids depart, the field trip over.
Alone with her worries, she recalls
she's a teacher, a lover of children
and all children, broken or whole
are gifts from God.

The phone rings ...
It's time.
Time to meet her grandson—Chase will be his name.
She pictures him Chasing butterflies, bunnies, and basketballs
like any other child.
But heart surgery calls.
More complications, more worries, more stress.
The phone becomes her enemy.

The phone rings ...
"Mom, can you babysit?"
"Of course," she says.
Chase sits by the window
delights in sights and sounds outside.
Silent—he Chases words that may never come.

Instead, he smiles, he laughs, and he loves.
A blessing to her family,
she no longer Chases
what could have been.

Mae Glerum

I WAS A ...

I was a rat when the wind blew
I was a butterfly when the sun was out
I was a monkey when it was hot
I was a rain cloud when it rained
And
I was love when you needed it.

WATER

humans
we are like a funnel
in a water bottle
after you shake it a hundred times
we swirl
and then we
settle
   to
     a
       stop

Raya Gottesfeld

Untitled

The wind blows.
The sun shines.
The grass breathes.

Fish slide in the night, calmly.

The rose has a petal.
A stem has no petal.

In the fall
the leaves fall down.
The wind blows.

Cars drive in
the night.
Lights sparkle,
flash in the moonlight.

QUESTIONS

*Written while homeless
with his mom*

Who am I?
Where do I belong?
Do I have a home?
What color are my
eyes? What color
is my hair?
Do I even
have hair?
What type of
color clothes
do I wear?
Am I a boy or a girl?
I'm not sure, you tell
me. Or can you? 'Cause
I'm not even sure if
I exist.

Courtlyn Helder

BLOWING A KISS TO MY SISTER

My hand went up to my eyes
getting wide as I laid a soft kiss
on the palm of my hand.
I lowered my hand, forming a 90 degree angle,
and then supporting it on my bony chin
I watched my sister do the same,
revealing her beaming face.
As we blew our flower petal
kisses off our hands,
prepared to catch each other's,
and gobble up the comfort wrapped within them,
the sting of wetness welled up in my eyes.
A dark storm cloud hovered over me,
giving me the unwanted worry of her safety
overseas in Uganda.
The loneliness of the cloud
gave me the thought
that this would be my last way to connect with her
for what would feel like the time it takes
to travel the whole world.

FROZEN SHADOWS

Why is a blade made?
Is it to attack or defend?
Is it for fact or pretend?
Why, in a game, is a gun so fun?
Is it the noise or the damage?
Is it for toys or a bandage?
Why must war be full of gore?
Can it not be spoken?
Or do bones have to be broken?
Are we bound to die from an explosion or erosion?
From age or rage?
From disease or overseas?

Remington Janssen

FAMINE

Famine sneaks from house to house,
Stealing essence
From sleeping bodies
Buried beneath heavy covers.
Creeping across snow covered fields
To feast on simple creatures
Pulsating in the cold.
Scarcity deprives abundance;
Pantries lack,
Fields want.
Hunger's work is done.
It prowls and slinks away.

Emma Faye Jewell

WHY SHOULD WE IN SOME FORGOTTEN CORNER

erasure from "Cosmos" by Carl Sagan

we are
        halfway to the
galaxy
                                        within
      are   worlds and
things   beings   civilizations

        seashells   corals
Nature laboring for aeons
        some hundred billion   galaxies each with
        a hundred billion stars
    In the face of
                       the Sun
            Why should we   in some
forgotten corner
                    brimming over with life
        do not yet know   beginning our explora-
tions   we are hard pressed

                the only planet
                utterly lost
    our journey   on Earth

  sparse   obscure   unpretentious
        seen   in the
                huge pinwheel of stars

                              spiral
arms turning slowly   Now
        we find ourselves falling
    an obscure

                        impression
            stars streaming by us   a vast array
        luminous stars

                                                        others

                    solitary

UNTITLED

the moon behind the clouds—
all these little old ladies

Skylar Kendall

THE PANGOLIN'S LOVE STORY

I fell in love at the farmer's market
With the prettiest pangolin the world has seen.
Her scales were lovely, so plump and smooth.
They shined with a polished gleam, deep green.

I was knocked back by her elegance,
a blast of pure gorgeousness.
Her olive scales, her lovely sheen!
I had to befriend that miss.

My legs wiggled like jelly,
as I inched towards the beautiful girl.
My cheeks turned to a bright red,
and my heart fluttered and twirled.

I finally managed to say "Hello,"
And ask her, "What's your name?"
I eagerly awaited her answer
But alas, no reply came.

I told her of my life in India
escaping famished trackers.
I escaped losing my scales for medicine
And being served with crackers.

I hid away upon a boat
To avoid those terrible straits.
I slipped into the cargo hold
To fend off those dreadful fates.

Within about a week,
I arrived at Fisk Mill Cove.
I rushed to the market to find some food,
And there I found my love.

Once I finished telling my story,
my girl just sat there like a rock.
She didn't budge a single inch,
And she didn't make a sound or talk.

"Mademoiselle, are you okay?
Is everything alright?
Maybe you're hungry,
so I'll go get us a bite."

I walked over to the nearest anthill
and picked up some ants to munch.
I laid them at the lady's feet,
but she didn't seem to want lunch.

I took a closer look at her,
but I couldn't find her eyes or tail.
And then it dawned on me that green
is not the normal color of our scales ...

I fell in love for the first time—
but it was all a joke.
The love of my life turned out to be
a ripe globe artichoke.

I took the artichoke home,
and I ate it with some chips.
That artichoke didn't make a good girlfriend,
but it sure made a good dip!

Stephanie Lester

THE TIRED FACE OF THE MAGICIAN RESCUES UNTRUTHS

With the threads
Of his footprints
He sets the darkness
As his wispy figure fades
Into his final act
The sounds of traffic burning
Their flickering headlights
His life's ambitions

Graham Linthorst

SUMMER

Summer is like eating cotton candy.

Summer eats candy apples,
it drinks lemonade.

It is friends with spring, winter, and fall.

Practically perfect summer
walks along slow, salty, smooth sand of beach.

Summer is a month of joy,
a month of everything you could ever think of.

The trees blow through the wind.
The trees shiver.
Leaves blow in the wind.
Suddenly leaves start to fall.
They fall deep,
from high to low,
slow or fast to the ground.

I hear the waves crashing and rolling.
They are high, medium or low.
Sometimes they are slow,
and sometimes they are fast.

I see children getting knocked off their boards
by the crashing waves.

I guarantee this is going to be
the best summer ever.

Madeline McEwen

A JOURNEY TO HEAVEN

Across the meadows
Over the deserts
Through the oceans
Onto the clouds
Under the trees
Beyond the valleys
Over the mountains
Past the cities
Towards my father
Towards his love
Towards the heaven that lies above

Bree, Liya & Anya Miksovsky

HAIKU

A bundle of sticks
warm in the cold.
Nest.
—Liya

Water gurgling, water splashing
rushing towards me and flowing away
as if it can't stand to sit still
—Liya

You know it's true
because I said it.
Write that down.
—Bree

a yellow orangey leaf
falls in front of me and joins
a pile on the ground
—Liya

pictures of bells
at midnight you can almost
hear their lovely sound
—Liya and Bree

a tiny depressing little ember
in the back of the fireplace
suddenly roars into life
—Anya

Liya and Bree
fight over a closet but then
I get to sleep there ha ha
          —Anya

Grandma meditates
while Liya and Bree screech
in their falling tent
          —Anya

CAT LOVE

Lick. Lick.
My cat's tongue is like sandpaper.
It's a nice sensation.
It feels like a warm kiss.
If my cat could talk I'd say, kissy, and he'd say, okay.
Then I'd ask, do you love me, and he'd answer, love is not divided.
It goes on forever.
I love you.
Lick. Lick.

Chloe Ortiz

CONFIDING WITH A HEN

I tell her
the rye truth.
We sit in the morning,
dew the soil staining.
She cocks her head,
I can tell she is listening.
Her small eyes
fill with tilled earth.
When I leave,
she pecks the ground,
searching.

TWINE: A PRAYER

God is a rope.
Long and thick,
it pulls us out of the water.
The roughness burns our skin.
We continue to climb, the waves
are still splashing. Our hands are red
and we shout to God.
We feel his leniency, strong and continuous.
Then, with a flick of his wrist,
we are flung back into the sea.

IN THE WOODS

I'm in the woods
I'm blending in
If I were in the woods
I'd totally blend in
If something was chasing me
I could just run in my shoes
They're super-fast runners
Maybe like a fox
Brown and white in the back
And white on the tail
It feels good because I
Could just blend into a tree
I would find a brown tree
And stand very still
Ready for anything under the sky!

Grace L. Park

THE POWER OF CLOTHES

I change from shorts to pantsuit, sweat left inside the car,
On top of the gym bag; careful steps in heels, not flip-flops.
People act the way they dress; skipping is impossible in suits.

DREAMING OF FRIENDS

A tiger in my dream chases me, and I wake cold in fear
My mother tells me that people don't give up when they love you.
I dream of the tiger again. This time, we become friends.

Lina Patel

LOST THINGS

We lose things all the time
socks in the laundry
hats
pencils
purses
library books
papers
coats
the grocery list
a stuffed animal
or even we lose
our senses
our temper
our minds
our heads
our hearts
our faith

But my question is
Where do those lost things go?
Does some magical force whisk them away
into a land of cake and candy?
Do future life forms transport them to another planet
with all the technology we haven't begun to discover?
Do they float into the clouds
visiting raindrops, twirling with snow?
Does a dragon with leathery wings and breath of fire
flap down to snatch them up with wide red jaws?
Do they just disappear?

Do we allow them to leave
through some subconscious decision?
Do they creep away themselves
stalking silently away from their owner?
Who, in the meantime

has looked everywhere
has just about had it
has to think of a better way
to find it

We sometimes get lost
misread the map
forget the directions
make a wrong turn
When that happens,
who has misplaced us?
who is our owner?
when will we be returned?

What happens
when lost things get forgotten?
replaced?
left behind?
Are they
still lost?

What happens
when you don't know something is lost?
and you're not worried?
not searching?
Is it
still lost?

Sometimes
if the lost thing is a part of you
you may never really get it back

My favorite part of losing things
is finding them again
after the long, deliberate hunt

and the search seems worthwhile
We finally discover their hidden location
like buried treasure

Sometimes the hidden home of what's missing
is hardly hidden after all
is really right in front of you
is somewhere that makes you say
"Oh!
Of course.
Why didn't I think of that before?"

Sometimes it takes only a little while to find lost things
sometimes it takes weeks
months
years
And you remember, after all the time
you remember losing it
you remember what it meant
you remember how you felt
like a dream
And you grasp it in your hand
and press it to your heart
and put it back where it belongs
Found.

Evie Portier

BEAUTY OF THE PRISONER

We sit side by side
watching the soul of yet
another day
dip into the darkness that swallows it whole.
Every.
Day.
The moment the sea latches
on
to our consciousness
we are pulled down.
Salt water pouring into our lungs.
Trying to kill
our
light.
We resist.
Thrashing through
arms
reaching at our legs
scratching open our calves.
The dunes become waves.
Crashing into our legs to prevent us from reaching
our destination.
We stop at the uppermost of the hill.
Panting in triumph.
Then we watch again,
as the prisoner is brought back
down.

ONCE UPON A TIME

Once upon a time there was an island,

and on that island, lived a dragon.

The dragon lived happy on that island,

until one day a man washed ashore.

So the dragon put him in the tower.

Then went to sleep.

THE ROCKS WERE SO TALL

The rocks were so tall, they touched
the sky. I would probably die if I climbed
one, but I climbed one anyway.
The wind howled and through
the throes of me. And I have no more to tell ...

Christell Victoria Roach

TRAILER PARK GIRLS

As children we dreamt of redemption,
the day when we'd leave this place.
Seclusion had no place in a child's world,
and the mountains of nothingness
held a loose embrace.

They say those are the days to remember
but now, with no welcome to the day,
I sit bound to my lawn chair,
awaiting the copper sun,
for I shall never leave this place.

Sabrina Swerdloff

OOPS

I watched
From my window
The bodies fall out.
I watched the bus
Slam, bang, crash
Into the side of
The Bay Bridge.
You were on the news,
One of the cadavers on the road
With no news headlines to tell.
The driver was on the news as well,
Babbling about "brake failure"
And "petrol leak" but
Really it was a careless swerve
A gas tank being crushed
And fire everywhere.
Really it was a mistake,
A momentary loss of balance,
A big yellow bus
Slam, bang, crash,
Into the side
Of the Bay Bridge.
And as I watch from my window
The ambulance come,
Take you and the rest of them
Away,
I think to myself that maybe it was fate.
Some higher calling
That caused your blood to spill,
That caused the bus to turn rapidly,
123 miles per hour
You could have been home.
Some higher calling
That decided that
It would be that particular

Petrol tank to explode
And toss its inhabitants
Onto the tarmac like salad.
There were 16 channels broadcasting this
One for every other car
That had been affected.
They call this "collateral damage."
The news report
18 deaths, 4 injuries,
22 people on the bus
Not including the driver.
The driver
Was fine.

GIRL RISING

*inspired by Richard Robbins'
documentary*

Given away at the hands
of cold rock
tastes the bloody flesh of letters
torn from words.

Hair billows in the distance
taken captive because all she wanted
was a pencil,
stones are thrown at her spine.

Smells the word *no*
as soon as she sits
on the wind broken benches.
Keep out! they say.

They dispose of her brain
throw away desktops
and hands raised.
Men slap away the chalk dust dreams.

Body succumbs to shattered
glass. Battered head lies
ripped, left for the dogs
to eat away.

All of a sudden—

the soles of her feet tremble
as she listens to the chord
of a distant drum
inside her.

She transforms into a pillar,
holds up the frayed edges of the earth
allows her fingers to be sodden with graphite
and erases scars at her mouth.

She lays pavement to new road
allows herself to sleep
on dreams about fever-pitch
that harvest paper

to write her tale where
the dirt is still trodden heavy
with cologne-soaked lies.
A new kingdom is brewing

where lips whisper
girl

rise
rise

rise.

PAST

We learned.
She taught me.
Taught me the secrets of the past.

Honest Abe.
Washington's wig.
Civil War.

We looked. And found the things that nobody else could.

Alone I am smart.
Together we are brilliant.

We packed our heads with unheard-of knowledge.

Until it was time to go.

She said we would see each other soon.

But that is my biggest worry.
I don't want to look into her past if she is not there to do it with me.

Junuh Tolan

EVENING TREES

Holding my father's hand
Telling me his side of the story
Helping me up on the wall
Telling me the war of the trees
And the wind
Trees falling
Wind dropping hearts stopping
Helping each other up not knowing
Wind is on the attack
Birds rushing to the water
Feathers flying
Sneezing people
Birds falling
Right back to the ground

SEE YOU AT HOME

Click. He opens the garage
door.
ZOOM! He flashes down
the hill
waving
Bye.
It opens
my heart.

Jamie Uy

EXPLAIN SUNBEAMS!

look here.
my hands are golden spirals carrying
color across the sky canvas.
i'm painting my dreams in yellow,
packing them into galaxy-black cellophane
and attaching them onto
lanterns of daylight.
my mother the Sun sends them up
into the comets' hidey-holes
as gifts to the solar system
on the coldest days of the year.

Peyton Vernon

NOBODY LIKES ME

I don't know why girls do not like me.
I still wear pink dresses,
They are pretty and sparkly and have crystals on them.
This night I saw a fairy godmother.
When she came in, I made my wish.
My wish was to be a fairy.

In the morning I spread magic everywhere.
Soon people started to like me.
So I put pixie dust on everyone.

Tabitha Welch

INSPIRATION

Sometimes I think
Inspiration is dead.

Other times
It jumps in my head.

It can be a friend
But also a traitor.

I suppose it's Fate.
Her.

Always something new
No two alike.

Middle of day,
Dead of night.

IN THE FOREST

In the forest
a man sits
a tree stands high
a river runs through his silence.

E. Wen Wong

DEAF CHILD, SWEET SOUND

Until one summer
they said I was deaf
I didn't listen
I couldn't
even if I wanted to.

Until one summer
they said I was quiet
I didn't listen
I couldn't
even if I wanted to.

Until one summer
they said I was daft
I didn't listen
I couldn't
even if I wanted to.

One summer
they said I was kind
I listened
what a sweet sound
I could hear.

Fiona Lauradunn Woolf

MYSTERY STORY

You're sitting in Mrs. Cuftor's house
You're drinking a glass of tea
The unknown is the door behind you that leads to someplace mysterious
And you're wondering about the humming on the deck
And the piano playing without fingers
And the sound of typewriting
You hear dark music from the mysterious door behind you
You take the cup of tea away from your lips
You stand up, and Mrs. Cuftor says
Stay awhile ...

Tianyue Xia

I WANT TO TELL THE FISH

I want to tell the fish,
Eat only the bait,
   not the hook.
When you eat the bait,
   start from its edge and
   slowly gnaw
   bit by bit.
Never ever gobble it in one go.

Contributor Notes

Contributor Notes

Why do you like writing poetry?

GWEN ALLISON: "I like to write poetry because I like to create feelings and pictures with words."

SAVANNAH ALVAREZ: "Because it lets me get my feeling out."

ELLIOT L. ARMITAGE: "When I write poetry, I feel like I empty myself and then I can start myself anew."

CAILENA BICKELL: "What's [poetry], again? I'm just good at talking."

GAVIA BOYDEN: "I like writing poetry because in it I can express my emotions freely, emotions which I would have trouble saying aloud. I also write poems because I like the feeling of writing."

OSCAR BRADY: "Poetry is interesting. It can be about real life or imaginary worlds; it can have a bit of humour or it can be serious … poetry can be anything you want it to be and that is why I like it."

ARIANE BRANIGAN: "I enjoy writing poetry because it's very versatile, and open to interpretation. There are no rules, no guidelines, no limitations. It has introduced me to other writers of my age who I identify strongly with, and who have helped me become more confident in my writing."

THEO CANDLISH: "I like to write poetry because it makes reading fun."

ABIGAIL ROSE CARGO: "I enjoy writing poetry because it comes naturally. I get an image in my head, add description, and I love feeling the words come together."

LAUREN E. CARTER: "I was sitting in front of my computer screen for a good half-hour trying to figure out how to answer this question in the most creative, professional, and impressive way possible. The longer I sat there, the more I realized I could only say the truth. To be honest, I barely write poetry. In fact, 'A Girl of Five or Eight's Exemplum' was a school assignment in which the directions simply stated 'tell a story.' So I did. I quite literally just wrote, made sure it flowed nicely, and printed it, along with some others, hoping it stood out."

RUBIO JETT CASTAGNA-TORRES: [to his father] "Because *you* are a poet and it's fun."

FRANK COLASACCO: "I like to write and I like to type funny stuff."

KATHMANDU COOK: "I like to write poetry because I love the words."

JAMES DAILEY: "Poetry allows me to write whatever I want unless I am in school."

JO'LENE DAILEY: "I love poetry because when you are home schooled or at home, you can talk about anything you want, like ponies. Because ponies are great and poetry is nice."

ZEA EANET: "I'm not sure; maybe because it's very freeing? There are so many different ways to write poetry, and they all open up different ways of expressing emotion, complex or simple."

KOFI EDUFO: "I write poetry to discover and learn the world inside and outside me. My father writes and reads mostly poetry. He tells us all the things happening in a poem. He shows us photographs and lives of poets. I have developed an interest in poetry and literature. I cannot sit down waiting and watching. That's why I write poems to amuse myself, making a poetry book to be part of the countless poetry books in the house."

ZEENA EL GINDI: "Poetry lets me express myself in ways that maybe others don't understand. It's like my poetry book is my best friend—it's the only thing that I can tell all my secrets to and it accepts my opinions the way they are."

Phoebe Fischer: "I like to write poetry because I can express my feelings in a beautiful language. Poetry is an art: It can paint a picture in your mind. Poems are beautiful things."

Aaron Fox: "I love words, a lot of sounds that those guys talk."

Rose Foster: "Because I can write whatever I want. Be creative and stuff. You get to do whatever words you want. But they have to make sense."

Madeleine Gallo: "I like to write poetry because I've grown up all my life hearing poetry. I love it and it makes me feel good."

Piper Ginn: "Poetry allows me to take a small piece of life and make it more meaningful."

Mae Glerum: "Because it's fun. It is a little bit like musical theatre. I know people who write poetry so I thought I would do it, too."

Melody Goldiner: "Sometimes all you need is to be calm and poetry makes me feel calm inside. Poetry uses a certain kind of language where you switch words around, not like speaking. It makes it more like a riddle. It takes me to places. If it's a good poem, you can hear the stories inside the riddles."

Raya Gottesfeld: "I like to write poetry because it's fun and imaginative. My favorite part is when the piece of paper is blank because then I get to think."

Savion Harris: "I like to write poetry because it gives the reader something to think about. I write not to give the reader my opinion, but to fit their opinion in, and they can take it for themselves. It is not for me to tell what the meaning is. My poems are meant to give meaning to each individual reader, for the mind of a reader is wondrous."

Courtlyn Helder: "Writing has always been one of my strengths, so when I discovered poetry, I was opened up to a whole new world. I like this world because you write in a unique way. You get to use words to describe things in different and unusual ways."

JOREL HILL: "I like creating poems because they are more fun than other types of writing. I can express emotion in clever ways and make rhymes chime."

REMINGTON JANSSEN: "When I first started writing poetry, I thought it was 'different.' I didn't really like writing at all. My teacher, Matt, at the Nueva School, taught me that poems are the skeletons of story. You connect a pile of interesting bones together in a way that makes sense and moves fluidly. Now I enjoy creating 'stories' that stand out. 'Famine' was originally an assignment to create a winter holiday card to send to our families. I decided to change things up a bit."

EMMA FAYE JEWELL: "I like to write poetry because I can express myself freely and rhythmically. Being a musician, the sound of poetry is something I love. I am also an avid reader, so this poem was interesting for me to write since I sampled from published text to create something unique and totally different from what was originally there."

MIKEY KELSEY: "I like writing poetry because it's fun."

SKYLAR KENDALL: "I'm a musician, and writing songs is very similar to writing poetry. They both use rhythm and sound to create a certain feeling. Poetry is a way to express my thoughts, and to share a moment with anyone who reads my words. For this poem, I was trying to get people to think of pangolins, and make people laugh."

STEPHANIE LESTER: "I like to write poetry because it lets me write in my own language; it doesn't have to make sense to anyone but myself. What I imagine becomes reality on paper."

GRAHAM LINTHORST: "It feels good to write. It makes me imagine better."

MADELINE MCEWEN: "Every emotion, every feeling I have can be expressed with a word. But poetry isn't just words muddled in a sentence. It gives us beauty even when the world seems ugly. That is why I love it so much."

NATALIE BELLE NEAL: "I like to write poetry because it helps me express my feelings better than saying it. Poetry helps me tell people about what I like. For example, my poem 'Cat Love' helped me explain that I love cats."

CHLOE ORTIZ: "I like to write poetry because when I read a good poem, it makes me feel good and I smile. I would like to make other people feel good too."

IAN JASPER OSBORN: "I like to write poetry because I can say anything that comes to my mind."

GRACE L. PARK: "I find that my poetry is strongest when it's from my experiences. In fact, one of my favorite quotes is one by John Steinbeck, who said, 'A story to be effective [has] to convey something from the writer to the reader, and the power of its offering [is] the measure of its excellence. Outside of that, there [are] no rules.' These sijos are two of my attempts to capture some of my experiences and how they've affected me."

LINA PATEL: "When I write poetry, I always think of what E.B. White said in the beginning of Stuart Little, 'I wrote this story for the children and to please myself.' And that's how it feels to write poetry for me, too."

ALEXANDER PROKOPIEV: "I like to draw because when I show my pictures to people, I feel satisfied when I see people become happy because of my hard work. That's what I enjoy mostly in life—making people smile. I also enjoy creating new characters, creatures, and worlds that no one has ever seen. I don't think of myself as a poet, admittedly. However, I do appreciate the fine art that is poetry. I think when I write, I have more time to think. Because of this, I am able to articulate my words in such a manner that it becomes fantastically extravagant ... I like to write because through my writing, I am able to communicate to other people. It is an important skill to have since we humans are such social creatures."

CHRISTELL VICTORIA ROACH: "I'm a young artist who always knew I was such. I grew up with stencils, paintbrushes, instruments (the infamous recorder, and viola), and leotards, too—but of all the arts I've dipped my toes into, the artist in me rests assured that writing is my forte. My sole desire is to move someone through poetry, and allow for my voice to be heard."

M. T.: "Poetry is like water—it's necessary to live."

MAXIMILIAN TELLINI: "I like poetry because it gives me a chance to express myself and the world in very beautiful, artistic way. It lets me release my feelings about things, and it helps me calm down and meditate when there is chaos in my life. And of course, I like it because it sounds amazing and soothing to the human ear."

JUNUH TOLAN: "In a poem I add onto what already happened with words and details. Those words and details give me that experience and add things from my imagination that surprise me and turn that experience into something else: a poem."

JACK URNESS: "Writing poetry lets me use my imagination."

JAMIE UY: "I like to write poetry because I get to figure myself out line by line. Coming up with clear images to accurately capture the feel of the poem is like fishing in a lake of my own experiences and emotions."

PEYTON VERNON: "I just love to write and tell stories. I think they make people really happy."

TABITHA WELCH: "I love to tell stories. A poem tells a story just like a short story or a novel does. Sometimes the poem can be much more artistic or dramatic. I think it is amazing that the same ideas that writers spend entire books exploring can be conveyed in a few poetic stanzas."

Ben Wilson: "I like writing poetry because it makes me feel like I am in another world and I forget about the normal world."

E. Wen Wong: "I think of poetry as an art to transfer our thoughts about the world, or imagination that lives around us, onto paper. It's as if we can connect with an audience through poetry by implementing surprises, unique stanzas, or even a single special word to catch their attention. Lastly, in my view, our minds are search engines constantly producing ideas to make an impact on the world, whether it is big or small."

Fiona Lauradunn Woolf: "I like to write poetry because it doesn't have to make sense. And if you're having something bad that is happening, you can write about it. And a poem can be almost anything. You could make it lyrics to a song, or you could make it words to a story. But the main reason I like to write poetry is because you're putting your feelings on a blank piece of paper and you can express yourself however you want."

Tianyue Xia: "Poems are beautiful. When I want to share a secret with a friend and don't want others to know it, I can say it in the poem. I like Su Dongpo best among all the ancient Chinese poets. He wrote the greatest poem about the moon. And I'm the moon. I like Du Fu, too, because I can understand his poems."

Some young poets chose not to include a note.

Rattle Young Poets Anthology
Guidelines

1) Poems must be submitted by a parent or legal guardian. We would be happy to have teachers encourage their students to submit work, but the submission itself must come from a parent.

2) The author of the poem must have been age 15 or younger when the poem was written, and 18 or younger when submitted.

3) The poets may use their whole name, first name, or a pseudonym at their parents' discretion. We will not publish any contact information.

4) Submit up to five poems at a time. Wait until we've replied to the first submission before sending more.

5) Upon acceptance, a parent or legal guardian must sign a release allowing us to publish the poem. We will also request an audio recording of the poem by the child for inclusion in the ebook version and/or on our website. Recording may be done yourself, or over the phone (we will provide details).

6) Only email submissions will be accepted. Include the parent/guardian's name and mailing address, and the child's age when the poems were written. The poems may be pasted into the body of a single email, or attached in a single file (.doc, .docx, .pdf, .rtf). Send the submission to:

children@rattle.com

Annual Deadline:
June 15